eMoTioN WeLL-BeinG

Tina Rae

@ebol

Published by **Atebol Cyfyngedig**, Fagwyr Buildings,
Llandre, Aberystwyth, Ceredigion SY24 5AQ
01970 832 172

www.atebol.com

ISBN: 978-1-907004-57-5

Project Managers: Colin Isaac and Glyn Saunders Jones
Editor: Colin Isaac
Design: Ceri Jones Studio, studio@ceri-talybont.com
Picture Research: Colin Isaac and Gill Saunders Jones
Funded by the Welsh Assembly Government
Printed by Gwasg Gomer, Llandysul, Ceredigion

Acknowledgements

The publisher wishes to thank Tina Rae for her enthusiasm and kindness during the preparation of these materials.

We would also like to thank Siriol Burford, Bedelia Dando, Mark Lancett (DCELLS), Heather Roy and Gareth Williams for their invaluable contributions during the preparation of these materials. Our thanks also to Teresa Carberry, Sian Harris, Mari Mitchell, Susan Rivers and Marilyn Webster who read or trialled the materials.

Finally, our thanks to Llinos Lanini for the photographs included on pages 39 and 53.

CONTENTS

WHAT IS WELL-BEING?

1 What is it?

The terms 'emotional well-being' and 'mental health' have similar meanings and implications. They are concerned with health of the mind, how we feel and think and how we view the world and make sense of what we see. People in good mental health have the ability to deal with and recover effectively from illness, change or misfortune.

2 What do you think?

- What makes people feel happy and well?
- What makes people feel unhappy and unwell?

Discuss the above questions and produce a definition of well-being.

KEY WORDS MENTAL HEALTH - WELL-BEING -

3 What about you?

Complete the self-check list on pages 6-7 in order to check some aspects of your well-being.

4 Activity

Ashley has been really fed up since he split up with his girlfriend Danielle. This was his first relationship and he had fallen for her in a big way. She finished with him because she said he was too intense and she wanted to have other relationships. She felt trapped and too young (at 15) to 'settle down'. She's started going out with someone else.

How are they both feeling now?

WORK IN A GROUP AND CHOOSE SOMEONE TO MAKE A NOTE OF YOUR ANSWERS

5 Follow-on

- · 'Young Minds' works directly with children and young people. Visit their website **www.youngminds.org.uk** and download leaflets and booklets for young people which may interest you.
- · You may wish to feedback in the next session regarding your work on the self-check list.

RESS/DISORDER - HEALTHY/UNHEALTHY OPTIONS

ACTIVITY SHEET

Self-Check List – Your Well-Being

Tick the box next to the statement you feel most accurately describes **YOU**!

1   I would describe myself as:

   a quite a happy and contented person who can cope with life's ups and downs ☐

   b rather a serious person who worries a bit but is relatively contented ☐

   c upset, agitated and irritable most of the time ☐

2   I generally feel that:

   a good things tend to happen to me and I'm hopeful about my future ☐

   b I find myself worrying quite a lot about the future ☐

   c I feel that I have few choices in my life and things are more likely to get worse than better in the future ☐

3   I would describe myself as:

   a sociable and confident, with lots of good friends ☐

   b sometimes finding it hard to talk to my friends – especially when things are difficult ☐

   c not having many close friends and sometimes not knowing where to turn ☐

4 Generally, I cry:

a if something happens that makes me feel very sad ☐

b relatively easily as I can be a little sensitive sometimes ☐

c very easily and often I will cry without knowing why ☐

5 Mostly my sleep is:

a good and I wake up feeling refreshed and energised ☐

b quite good but sometimes I find it hard to get to sleep and I wake up early ☐

c disturbed because I don't sleep well or for long enough or I sleep all the time ☐

6 When I have a lot going on in my life:

a I try and keep a balance and still see my friends or do other things I enjoy ☐

b my friendships and social activities tend to suffer ☐

c I hide myself away ☐

How did you do?

Mostly a's – you are able to look after yourself well and know when and how to get help. You can talk about your feelings and make sure that you keep a balance between work and social activities. You just need to keep monitoring yourself and set realistic targets in order to maintain your well-being.

Mostly b's – you sometimes feel overwhelmed and don't take care of your emotional and physical needs. You need to make a well-being plan for yourself, identifying strategies to keep well and others who can help you.

Mostly c's – you are finding life difficult and feel overwhelmed the majority of the time. Talk to a parent/friend or a mentor/counsellor about these problems and start to develop some self-help strategies. Research top tips for positive mental health and begin to make a plan.

COPING WITH CHANGE

1 What is it?

For most young people, the greatest changes they experience occur during the first 5 years of secondary education. The transfer from the more intimate primary school to the larger high school can be frightening for many. The physical and emotional changes that occur during puberty can also cause high levels of anxiety. It is important for young people to understand that these changes are all a part of 'normal' development and to develop appropriate ways of coping with them.

2 What do you think?

- What do you think are the main changes experienced by young people?
- Are these negative/positive changes?
- How did you deal with them?
- What worked best for you?

WORK IN GROUPS AND THEN FEEDBACK

KEY WORDS CHANGE - PUBERTY - PHYSICAL - EMOTIONAL - ANXIET

3 What about you?

If you were asked to change 3 things about yourself now, what would you change and why? What would help you to change and who might support you?

INDIVIDUAL SELF-REFLECTION ACTIVITY

4 Activity

Complete the change scenarios activity on pages 10-11.

WORK IN PAIRS

5 Follow-on

Leigh's Mum and Dad were divorced last year. The mother has just moved in with a new man called Glyn. Leigh thinks he's okay but can't stand his two children. They are twins aged 15 and are used to having everything they want and doing things their own way. Leigh is quite quiet and shy and likes to have privacy – especially as the GCSE mocks are coming up. The twins keep taking stuff from Leigh's room and playing their music really loud. Leigh feels unable to cope with this change in lifestyle. What would you advise?

NORMAL DEVELOPMENT - NEGATIVE RESPONSES - POSITIVE RESPONSES

Change Scenarios

1 Read through each of the 10 imaginary scenarios opposite. Rate each of them from 1 to 10 according to how stressful it might be for you.
(1 would be 'really stresses me out' and 10 would be 'doesn't stress me at all'.)

2 Choose the scenario that would stress you most and your partner should do the same. Discuss these 2 choices with your partner.

3 Match each of the scenarios with the most appropiate support system given in the third column.

Rating	Scenario	Support Systems
	Someone you love has been diagnosed with terminal cancer.	Find out about support from Alcoholics Anonymous
	Your brother/sister has decided he/she is gay and wants to come out.	Discuss with friends and find out how they cope
	Your Mum has decided to divorce your Dad.	Find out what help is available from Stonewall
	Your friend is getting into drugs and it is making him/her quite aggressive.	Talk to a Marie Curie professional
	You continually argue with your Mum because she treats you like a little kid and won't let you have any freedom.	Contact an information and advice service for young people, e.g. Drug Aid Wales/Connexions
	Your step-dad is acting weird around you and keeps trying to touch you in an inappropriate way.	Look up Gam - Anon online and see what help is available
	Your Dad has just lost his job and he's started drinking heavily.	Tell her to talk to your GP
	Your sister who is 15 has just told you that she's pregnant.	Talk to the school counsellor
	You are a refugee seeking asylum in this country as there is a war in your country.	Talk to your child protection officer at school
	Your Mum has become addicted to gambling and is spending most of her money on this – to the extent she can't afford the weekly food shop.	Contact the Refugee Council

CODING WITH STRESS

1 What is it?

The word 'stress' covers a wide range of things, most of which appear to be unpleasant to the individual/group concerned. There is, however, agreement that stress can be caused by a significant increase in pressure without the necessary strategies or resources to cope with this.

2 What do you think?

- What causes you stress?
- In groups, discuss your 'stressors' (factors that cause you stress) and make a list of the most common stressors.
- As a class, choose 5 of these stressors and for each arrange yourselves in a line according to how big a stressor this is for you – stand at the start of the line if this is a big stressor for you or towards end of the line if it is less important in your life. Do this for each of the 5 stressors chosen.

KEY WORDS STRESS - CODING STRATEGIES - KEEP?

3 Activity

Prepare your own stress profile using the table on page 14.

4 What about you?

Here are some stressors for young people:

- You feel you are not good enough.
- You feel worried about the future.
- You don't feel like a complete person.
- You feel you need adults to help out too much.
- You find it hard to set limits for yourself.
- You feel unsure about your sexuality.
- You find it hard to make and sustain important relationships.
- You find it hard to cope with your emotions.
- You find it hard to accept responsibility.

Chose one of these stressors you have experienced, i.e. one each, and discuss them:

- How did you cope?
- What helped you?
- How are your strategies similar/different?

5 Strategies for coping with stress

Keeping fit, meditation, relaxation, prioritising & problem solving are some of the useful strategies for coping with stress. Do some research using the internet and/or other sources and produce a list of 10 useful ways of coping with stress. (Useful sites include: **www.meiccymru.org**; **www.getconnected.org.uk** and **www.youth2youth.co.uk**). Which of these would you use and which wouldn't you use?

6 Follow-on

Design a mind map for coping with stress. (See page 15.) Work in groups and focus on a particular set of strategies e.g. exercise, meditation, alternative therapies etc.

FIT - MEDITATION - RELAXATION - PRIORITISING

Stress Profile

How stressed do you feel? Read each statement, then tick the relevant box.

DO YOU.....	All the time	Most of the time	Sometimes	Not often	Never
Have headaches					
Feel up and down					
Lack concentration					
Not want to see friends					
Get irritable					
Feel anxious					
Bunk off school					
Feel fed up					
Blame yourself					
Feel tired					
Feel sick and wound up					
Overeat					
Lose your appetite					
Think things are pointless					
Get angry					
Feel undermined by others					
Lack confidence					
Feel lonely/isolated					
Drink too much					
Argue with others					
Feel tearful					
Forget things					
Feel dependent on drugs					
Have nightmares/bad dreams					
Keep your problems secret					
Have stomach aches					
Keep swallowing					
Have sweaty hands					
Clench your fists					
Feel a lump in your throat					

If most of your ticks are in the first 2 columns then you are probably experiencing an unhealthy level of stress in your life.

You need to seek advice and support and work out an Anti-Stress Action Plan for yourself (see next page).

Actually an Anti-Stress Action Plan is something everyone would find beneficial.

Ideas for coping with stress

BUILDING MOTIVATION

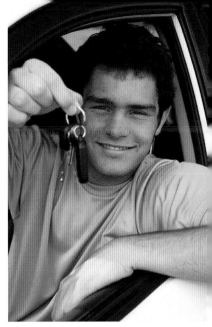

1 What is it?

Motivation is necessary if you are to bring about change in your lives. It's necessary for you to believe that change is important and have confidence that you will be successful. 'Self-motivation' is what allows you to change and develop – rather than other people telling you how to change and why you should do so.

2 What do you think?

- How would you describe motivation?
- What motivates you?
- Do people who are important in your life (parents, peers, teachers) share your motivators?
- How do you cope when you don't share the same goals?

> WORK IN GROUPS AND THEN FEEDBACK

KEY WORDS MOTIVATION - SELF-MOTIVATION - CHANGE - RELAPSING - NEG

3 The change cycle

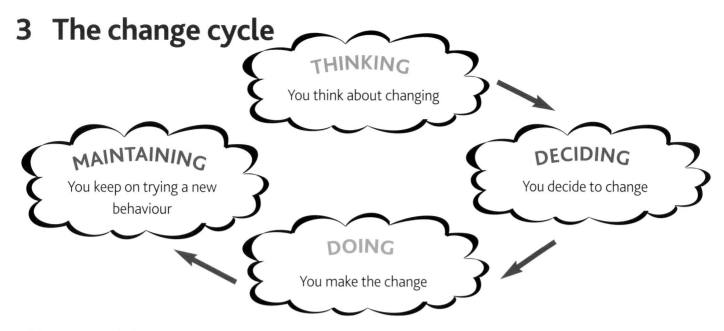

THINKING
You think about changing

DECIDING
You decide to change

DOING
You make the change

MAINTAINING
You keep on trying a new behaviour

A fifth cloud would be: RELAPSING – it goes wrong and you return to the old behaviour. Where would this cloud go?

4 Activity – Ceri's Problem

Ceri is overweight and is trying to do something about it (Stage 3 of the Change Process). Ceri has tried to do this in the past but always turns to food when upset.
How can Ceri get to Stage 4 and maintain a healthier lifestyle?
What advice would you give to Ceri?
Draw up an ACTION PLAN (including strategies and support systems).

WORK IN GROUPS AND THEN FEEDBACK

5 Follow-on

* Complete the Activity Sheet on pages 18-19.

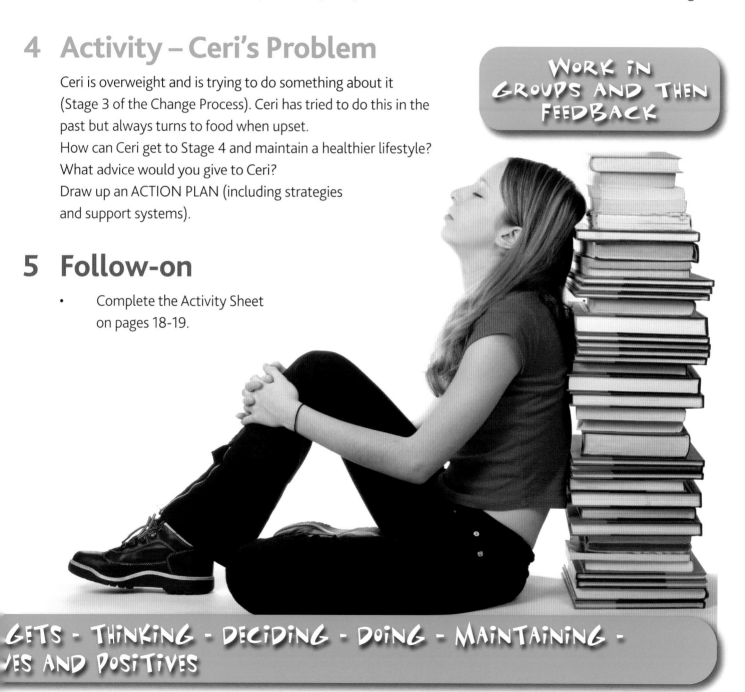

GETS - THINKING - DECIDING - DOING - MAINTAINING -
/ES AND POSITIVES

Motivated or Not? – What about you

- Think of something in your life that you would like to change. Examples may include:
  - Being happier
  - Improving your appearance
  - Having a boyfriend/girlfriend
  - Being less stressed
  - Stopping smoking
  - Getting fit
  - Drinking less
  - Working harder

- List the positives and negatives for making this change.

POSITIVES I want to do this because:	NEGATIVES I don't want to do this because:

- Think of 3 things you can do in the next week to begin to make this change and set yourself some realistic targets.

- Fill in the change cycle below in relation to the change you are trying to make. Add a cloud for 'relapsing' if appropriate.

LEARNING TO LISTEN

1 What is it?

Being able to listen is an essential skill in building good relationships with others.
Communication involves 2 parts: speaking and listening – or sending and receiving a message.

2 What do you think?

- Why do we need to listen?
- What would happen if people didn't bother to develop listening skills?

> DISCUSS IN GROUPS AND FEEDBACK TO SEE IF YOU CAN AGREE ON YOUR DESCRIPTIONS

KEY WORDS LISTENING - POSTURE - COMMUNICATION - FACIAL EXPRESSION - BODY LANG

3 Listening experiment

- You will a need a blank sheet of paper and a pencil
- Your teacher is going to read out some instructions
- Listen very carefully and follow each instruction in turn
- Look at your results! How well did you listen?

4 Activity

Look at the Top Tips for Good Listening on page 22 and think of these during this activity.

Work in 3's. Nominate 1 person (A) to choose a topic about which to talk and give them 3 minutes to think about this.

The other 2 (B and C) can look at the top tips.

After the 3 minutes A will talk about the chosen topic, B will listen and C will observe to see how well B listens to A.

Remember to look at: posture, voice, eye contact, personal space, gestures, facial expression, head movements and hand movements.

DISCUSS What did the listener do well? What do they need to improve?

SWAP ROLES and try again.

After discussing the second listener's performance, **SWAP ROLES** and try again.

5 Follow-on

- Look again at the Top Tips on page 22, then answer the questions at the bottom of that page.
- Complete the Listening Behaviour Checklist shown on page 23. Be as honest as you can and then analyse your responses. What skills do you need to develop further?

CONTACT - OPEN NOT CLOSED QUESTIONS - GESTURES -
SE - CLARIFICATION - INTERRUPT

Top Tips for Good Listening

**React
and use short words of
encouragement**
Show you're listening by nodding and using short words – "mmm" "yes" "I see" "Go on".

**Show
positive body language**
Be relaxed but show you're concentrating on what's being said. For example, relax your arms, don't cross them.
Sitting slightly forward and tilting your head means you're listening.
Lots of eye contact, but don't stare.
Smiles and nods but only where appropriate.

**Be
sympathetic**
Comments like "That must have been difficult" and "Sounds like you've had a bad time" can help.

**Listen
and look for clues**
What have they been feeling?
Did they mention something in passing which they're hoping you'll ask more about?

**Use
open, not closed, questions**
Use questions starting with 'How', 'What', 'Where', 'Why' and 'Who' to encourage your friend to talk.
What's happening now?
How do you feel about…?
Closed questions need one-word answers and can stop a conversation flowing.
Was he angry? – Yes.

**Show
you understand**
Do this by summarising what they've said. If you don't understand, ask them to clarify or repeat it differently: So do you mean…?

**Don't
say too much**
Sometimes listening or even just being there with them is enough. They may just need to talk and not want your advice.

**Don't
be afraid to ask**
If they don't want to talk about it they'll say so. Then you respect their choice and leave it at that for the moment.

- Think of a time when you have not listened well. Which of these Top Tips were not used?
- Think of a time when you listened well. Which of these Top Tips did you use?

Listening Behaviour Checklist

Rate your own listening skills using the following scale:

4 = Always   3 = Most of the time   2 = Sometimes   1 = Never

I look the speaker in the eye when he/she is talking	1 2 3 4
I look interested even if the subject bores me	1 2 3 4
I wait for the speaker to finish before responding	1 2 3 4
I keep an open mind and do not respond negatively to the speaker's ideas or feelings.	1 2 3 4
I do more listening than talking	1 2 3 4
I give the speaker my full attention (not look at my watch, fidget, do something else at the same time)	1 2 3 4
I use good non-verbal responses e.g. nodding, smiling, leaning forward	1 2 3 4
I give brief verbal responses e.g. Uh-huh, Mmm	1 2 3 4
I ask for clarification if I am unsure about what has been said	1 2 3 4
I try to understand the speaker's feelings	1 2 3 4

Now add up your score!   Total =_____

How did you score?

10-19   Your listening skills need to improve. Look carefully at the checklist and note the key areas that need improvement. Get practising – you'll soon notice an improvement.

20-30   You're doing well but there's still room for improvement. Look at the checklist to see where you can improve.

Over 30   Congratulations! You're already an excellent listener. See if there are any areas you could improve on further.

My Action Plan
To be a better listener I will:

_____

Practise over the next week and keep a diary in which you record progress.

CODING WITH LOSS AND BEREAVEMENT

1 What do you think?

What is loss?

Discuss in the whole group. Your teacher will then make a list of the different types of loss you have mentioned. Discuss how these are similar and how they are different.

2 Helpful or unhelpful

Think about how someone might feel and behave when they have recently lost someone they loved. You will be given a set of cards, with each card containing a statement of something which could be done in such a situation. In your groups sort these into 2 piles: things that would be helpful and things that would be unhelpful.

KEY WORDS LOSS - GRIEF - BER

3 The grief cycle

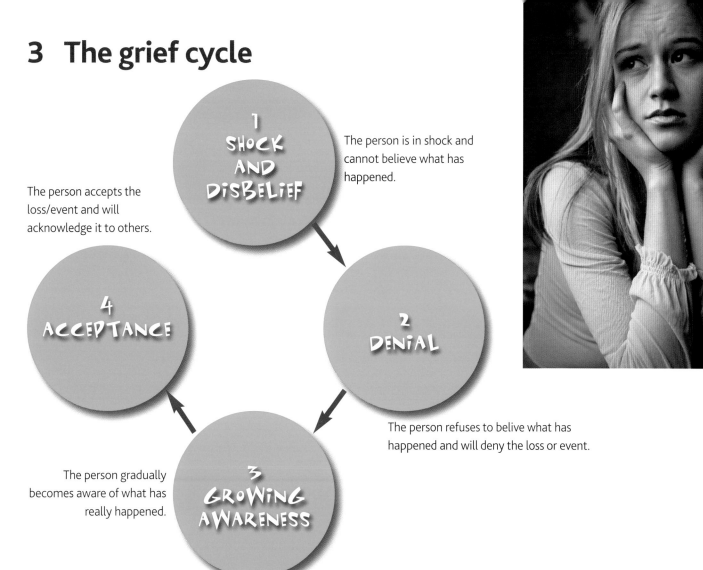

The person is in shock and cannot believe what has happened.

1 SHOCK AND DISBELIEF

The person accepts the loss/event and will acknowledge it to others.

4 ACCEPTANCE

2 DENIAL

The person refuses to belive what has happened and will deny the loss or event.

The person gradually becomes aware of what has really happened.

3 GROWING AWARENESS

A 5th point is anger. The person may experience feelings of anger at each stage of the cycle. They also may feel sadness, pain, isolation, fear and other painful emotions.

4 Activity

Complete the Grief Cycle on page 27 in relation to a young person who is facing bereavement or a break-up of his parents' marriage. How do you think that person would

- think
- feel
- act

INDIVIDUAL ACTIVITY

at each stage?
What strategies could be used?

5 Follow-on

- Investigate helpful organisations and agencies which may help young people and adults who have experienced a bereavement or are expecting a bereavement. Some examples are given below. Make a display of information leaflets, brochures and on line resources.

Bereaved Parents Network – Care for the Family

Garth House, Leon Avenue, Cardiff CF15 7RG

Tel: 029 2081 0800

The Child Bereavement Charity

Aston House, West Wycombe, High Wycombe, Buckinghamshire HP14 3AG

Tel: 01494 678088

The Compassionate Friend

53 North Street, Bristol BS3 1EN

Helpline: 0845 123 2304

Cruse Bereavement Care

Cruse House, 126 Sheen Road, Richmond

Surrey TW9 1UR

Winston's Wish

Gloucestershire Royal Hospital, Great Western Road, Gloucester GL1 3NN

Tel: 01452 394377

Email: info at winstonswish.org.uk

Website: www.winstonswish.org.uk

- There are many different ways to celebrate someone's life. These include:
    * Making up memory books
    * Designing and making up special photograph albums
    * Writing cards
    * Making a tape
    * Creating a memory poster of a special day
    * Making up a tape of special music that the person loved
    * Making a memento box in which there are lots of trinkets or special things that the person loved or owned

Think of someone special to you and make up your own memory book to celebrate their qualities and the reasons why you would miss them if they were no longer with you.

The Grief Cycle

1
SHOCK AND DISBELIEF

2
DENIAL

3
GROWING AWARENESS

4
ACCEPTANCE

SELF-HARM

1 What is it?

Each year literally thousands of young people are taken to hospital after trying to harm themselves. Of the young people who try to harm themselves, three out of every four are females. These young people may feel that they cannot cope with their circumstances and that they are totally unable to change these circumstances.

2 What do you think?

WORK IN GROUPS AND FEEDBACK

- What other names are used for self-harm?
- What are the most common forms of deliberate self-harm?
- Why do you think young people self-harm?

KEY WORDS SELF-HARM - DEPRESSION - SI

3 What about you?

There are many things people have said about self-harm including:

- It's attention seeking
- It's self-inflicted, so it's not serious
- It leads to suicide
- Only Goths and Emos self-harm
- If they won't see a psychiatrist then they can't want to get better
- Self-harmers are usually hysterical women under 25 who grow out of it

Do you agree with these statements? If so, why? If not, why not?

4 Activity – helping Josh who self-harms

Josh is 15 and is gay. He has known this since he was about 12 years old. He lives in the countryside and feels quite isolated as there is not much for young people to do. He recently confessed to a friend at school that he was anxious and lonely. That person has now started spreading rumours about him. Josh now feels sick at the thought of going to school. He knows he will get bullied and he starts to self-harm. What advice would you give him at this stage? Use the Activity Sheet on page 31 to record your answers.

WORK IN GROUPS AND FEEDBACK

5 Coping Strategies

Listed below are strategies some people use to try to reduce self-harming behaviours:

- Take a very hot shower
- Hold ice-cubes which have been dyed red
- Take exercise
- Listen to calming music
- Use a punch bag

WORK IN GROUPS

Discuss these strategies (and any others you may know) and suggest what may be positive and negative about each one.

-ESTEEM - GUILT - COPING STRATEGIES

6 Follow-on

Investigate the following help and advice lines and collect relevant and useful publications from each of them in order to make a display.

- Bristol Crisis Service for Women - it produces information and publications about self-injury and offers talks and trends to professionals. Helpline 0117 925 1119.

- Childline, www.childline.org.uk - a free 24-hour helpline for children and young people which also provides publications and fact sheets. Helpline 0800 1111.

- National Self-harm Network, www.nshn.co.uk - an organisation campaigning for the rights of understanding for people who self-harm.

- Samaritans, www.samaritans.org - provides confidential emotional support 24 hours a day. Helpline 0845 790 9090.

- Young Minds, www.youngminds.org.uk - the helpline for concerns about mental health for a child or young person. Helpline 0800 018 2138.

- Local support projects in your area. (Your teacher can give you contact details for these).

Helping Josh who self-harms

Below is a list of strategies that could be used to support Josh who self-harms. Place them in rank order using 1 for the most helpful strategy and 10 for the least helpful. In the final column record your reasons for your choices.

	Ranking	Reasons
Talk to him about it		
Tell a responsible adult		
Ask to see his injuries		
Find out more information from him		
Tell him to wear long sleeves to cover his injuries		
Encourage him to get professional help		
Offer to go with him to see a counsellor		
Tell all his other friends so that you can offer support together		
Tell him to stop it		
Listen to him		

SUICIDE

1 What is it?

Suicide is one of the main causes of death amongst teenagers. For every female who attempts to take their own life, there are approximately three males who do so. Young people who attempt suicide do not necessarily self-harm before this and do not always let others know of their intentions.

2 What do you think?

- What are the ways that young people tend to commit suicide?
- Why do young people take their own lives?
- What sort of support do they need? Where can they get help?

WORK IN GROUPS AND FEEDBACK

KEY WORDS SUICIDE

3 What about you?

INDIVIDUAL SELF-REFLECTION

What's your opinion about each of these statements regarding suicide?

- People who take their own lives are selfish
- Only sick people commit suicide
- If you are really depressed you are more likely to take your life
- If a close friend commits suicide you are more likely to do so too
- Websites that promote suicide for young people should be banned
- Young people need to talk about their problems to others who can help so they are not at risk

4 Activity

Amy's boyfriend has finished with her. She is heartbroken as they had planned to go off to college together. Recently, she has been accessing sites on the internet where there is information about committing suicide and making a pact with other people from around the world to do this. She is becoming obsessed with this and is beginning to feel that it must be a 'normal' thing to do if so many others are talking like this. She feels that her life isn't worth living now and that no-one would miss her being around.

If you were her friend what advice would you give her at this stage? Where could you both get help? What would you need to do?

WORK IN GROUPS AND FEEDBACK

5 Follow on

- Investigate the following websites and try to find out what are the best sources of support for young people at risk of suicide:

  www.mind.org.uk   www.repsych.ac.uk   www.nice.org.uk

- Complete the activity sheet 'Suicide and the Media' on pages 34-35.

DEPRESSED - SUPPORT

Read the following article:

Suicide and the Media

Local teenager, Jeff Coleman, took his own life last Wednesday. He had recently been asked to leave his school, where he was due to sit his 'A' levels. Staff stated that he was poorly behaved, rude and aggressive and recently had been caught cheating. He had apparently downloaded an essay from the internet and also had taken notes into a recent mid-term exam. He was found in his father's car having crashed it directly into the side of their garage. Apparently, shortly before his death he had gone to the school and begged the head teacher to give him a second chance. This had been refused and he was ordered to leave the premises, pending a permanent exclusion.

No hope

His best friend, Carl Rogers, said yesterday, 'The school is directly responsible for Jeff's suicide. They took away his hope and his future. They didn't even bother to find out why he was acting the way he was. I'd like the head to tell us how he feels now.'

Earlier this morning the head teacher, Edward James, gave the following statement: 'We are deeply saddened by what has happened but I don't think an absolute connection can be made between Jeff's exclusion and his death. We have had to discipline and permanently exclude other students in the past and none of them have gone on to take their own lives.'

No help

A neighbour and close friend of the family, Elin Hughes, said that Jeff had become increasingly moody during the last couple of months. 'I offered help several times but he didn't want to know. I spoke to his parents but they didn't want to know either. They told me to keep my nose out of things that didn't concern me. I'm not surprised this has happened. It's very sad but I'm afraid some of us could see it coming!'

Now complete the 'Reflection Chart'

Reflection Chart

Is any of the information in the article not based on facts? If so, what information?	
What opinion might a reader form about Jeff and his suicide from reading this article?	
Would you have written the article in a different way? If so, how and why?	

MANAGiNG ANGER

1 What is it?

According to psychologists it isn't what happens to us which makes us angry but rather the way we view the event. Therefore one way to control anger is to prevent the angry feeling developing by changing the way we view things.

2 What do you think?

Thoughts lead to feelings which lead to behaviours.

Try to remember a NEGATIVE THOUGHT you have had.
How did it make you FEEL?
How did it make you BEHAVE?
How could you have thought differently or interpreted another person's behaviour differently in order to stop the cycle of thoughts – feelings – behaviours?

iNDiViDUAL SELF-REFLECTiON ACTiViTY

Thoughts → Feelings → Behaviours

KEY WORDS THiNKiNG - FEELiNG - BEHAViOUR - TI

3 What about you?

Triggers are events which could lead to angry feelings. For each of the triggers given below suggest a thought which could lead you to be angry and a thought which could lead you not to be angry. Draw up a chart like this.

Triggers	Thought leading to anger	Thought not leading to anger
Someone pushes you over	They want to fight me	They lost their balance

TRIGGERS: Your best friend doesn't talk to you
You are told off for not completing coursework
Your friend calls you a liar
Your mother won't let you go to a party and you're the only one not going.

WORK IN SMALL GROUPS

4 Activity

The 'Stepped Approach' is one way of 'dampening the fuse' when a particular trigger event could have made you angry. The steps are:
1) Don't react immmediately - wait until you've calmed down a bit
2) Listen to the other person (even if you disagree)
3) Say how you feel clearly
4) Provide a solution – say how it could be better or different

Choose one of the anger triggers below. Working in pairs, act out the situation. Work out a positive response so that you dampen the fuse!

WORK IN PAIRS

- The teacher has accused you of stealing and it wasn't you.
- You've been left out of the team because the captain doesn't like you.
- An older student has made a racist comment to your best friend.
- Your best friend has gone off with someone else to a party and left you out.

5 Follow-on

- Do the Relaxation Exercise given on page 38. This can be done in different ways, which your teacher can explain.
- Think of a 'personal anger trigger', i.e. something that has really made you angry. Try to find a solution – a way of dealing with the situation without getting angry, perhaps by using the stepped approach.

GERS - RELAXATION SCRIPT - STEPPED APPROACH

ACTIVITY SHEET

Relax yourself!

Make a recording of the following script for your use. Then find a quiet, private space, play the recording and follow the instructions.

- Sit on a chair with your legs uncrossed and your hands on your lap, Close your eyes.

- Clench your fists, hold them tense, then relax them. Repeat this.

- Bend your elbows and tense your biceps, hold, then relax. Repeat.

- Frown and pull your forehead muscles together, hold, then relax. Repeat.

- Lift your shoulders, hold them tense, then relax them. Repeat.

- Press your feet on the floor and tense your calf muscles, hold, then relax. Repeat.

- Relax all over – from toes through to feet, ankles, calves, thighs, chest, shoulders arms and neck. Relax your jaw and face. BREATHE DEEPLY and let your breath out slowly.

- Count to 10 and open your eyes.

ASSERTIVENESS SKILLS

1 What is it?

It isn't always easy to make the distinction between being assertive and being aggressive. Many people who have low levels of self-esteem can often appear to be aggressive when they have to cope with difficult situations. Alternatively, they may become passive and withdraw from the problem.

Imagine you have to take a DVD back to the shop because it keeps jumping. Act it out in pairs. Do this in an assertive way, an aggressive way an a passive way.

WORK IN PAIRS

2 What do you think?

You will each be given three coloured cards. The red card represents 'aggressive', the green card represents 'assertive' and the blue card represents 'passive'.

Your teacher will read out the following statements (and others perhaps). After each statement lift up the card you think applies to that statement.

- If you don't do that I'll slap you.
- Get out of my way!
- Can you please listen to me?
- It's probably my fault.
- What do you think about this?
- I can't stand you!
- You had better change that or else…
- I don't know what to say.
- When can we talk about this?
- You're pathetic.
- I am listening to you so please listen to me.
- You idiot! Why did you do that?
- I'm feeling uncomfortable about this.

KEY WORDS SELF-ESTEEM - BEHAVIOUR - AGGRESSIVE - BO

3 Body language

As well as what we say, our body language can also make us appear aggressive, e.g. how we use our eyes and hands and don't allow others their personal space.

- Illustrate assertive and aggressive body language in pictures – either make your own drawings, cut out appropriate pictures from magazines or take photos to produce your illustrations.
- What labels could you add to your illustrations to help other people understand the distinction between assertive and aggressive body language?

4 Activity

In pairs, choose one of the following scenarios, work out an 'assertive script' for it and then act it out. Think carefully about the language and body language you use.

WORK IN PAIRS - ACT IT OUT

- Someone's pushed you in the queue.
- Someone's accused you of stealing from a shop and you didn't.
- Someone's taken your work and said they did it.
- Someone's told a lie about your best friend.

5 Follow-on

- Complete the Self-Check List on page 42, rating yourself out of 10 for each of the assertive and aggressive behaviours given. Be honest! Then analyse your skills – what do you need to do in order to become more assertive rather than aggressive?

- Think of a time when you responded aggressively to another person.
  - What led up to to your behaviour in this situation?
  - How did you behave in this situation?
  - What were the consequences of your behaviour?

  If you were in the same situation again, what would you do differently to get a better outcome? What would your assertive response be?

LANGUAGE - SELF-RESPECT - RESPECT - RESPONSIBILITY

ACTIVITY SHEET

Self-Check List

How assertive are you? Rate yourself out of 10 against each of the following descriptors:

BEING ASSERTIVE	BEING AGGRESSIVE
You listen properly to what other people are saying. /10	You are 'loud'. /10
You are honest about your thoughts and feelings to others. /10	You sometimes abuse others verbally/physically. /10
You are honest with yourself about your thoughts and feelings. /10	You can cause other people to feel upset. /10
You are sensitive towards other people. /10	You need to win even if others get hurt or upset. /10
You ask for what you want. /10	You put others down. /10
You take responsibility for your behaviour and the choices you make. /10	You force others to do things that they don't want to do. /10

Personal Reflection

Do you need to become more assertive? If so, think of ways in which you can achieve this goal. Set yourself some targets and at the end of each week check how well you are doing with regard to achieving those targets.

What do I need to do to be more assertive?

1

2

3

What will help me to achieve these targets?

1

2

3

CONFLICT MANAGEMENT

1 What about you?

WORK IN PAIRS

- When did you last have an argument?
- How did you feel?
- How do you think the other person felt?
- What was the outcome?
- How could you have achieved a better outcome for both parties?

2 What is it?

Conflict is a normal part of everyday life. Knowing how to resolve disagreements and difficult issues effectively are essential life skills which also protect emotional well-being. Resolving conflict requires individuals to respect another's viewpoint and to try to understand how they feel. One simple rule applies: aim for a win-win solution and avoid a lose-lose outcome at all costs.

- What skills do you currently use to resolve conflicts?

INDIVIDUAL SELF-REFLECTION ACTIVITY

KEY WORDS CONFLICT - SOLUTION - RESOLVE - AGREE -

3 What do you think?

WHOLE CLASS DISCUSSION

Here are some guidelines for resolving a conflict positively:

- Don't try to resolve a conflict if someone is still angry
- Don't keep on blaming each other
- Be honest about your part in the problem
- Try to see the problem from the other person's perspective
- Try to focus on solutions and choose the one that's nearest to a win-win

Suggest other guidelines which could help to resolve a conflict positively.

4 Activity

Jason isn't talking to his mum because she doesn't want him to go out every weekend. She thinks he's drinking too much and is putting his health at risk. He thinks she's over the top and neurotic and all his mates get drunk. She is really worried and he is angry and is now staying out later than ever just to annoy her.

How can they solve this conflict? Use the problem-solving format shown on page 46 and work through this stepped approach to try to find a win-win solution.

Alternatively make up your own conflict situation and use the stepped approach to try to find a solution.

5 Follow-on

- Peer mediation involves a student acting as a mediator, i.e. a 3rd party who tries to resolve a conflict between two other students. Complete the Activity Sheet on page 47.

- There is generally less conflict where there is more kindness! Focus on doing random acts of kindness in order to make your environment happier and healthier for everyone. Do at least one act of kindness every day for the next week. These don't have to be 'big' – think of things you could do to make others happy. When the week is over, stop and reflect. What difference did this make? How did you feel?

EN - RESPECT - WIN-WIN - RANDOM ACTS OF KINDNESS

Problem-solving Format

1. What's the problem? How does each person feel?

2. Who might help? What could they do?

3. What can each person do to help to solve the problem?

    Option 1

    Option 2

    Option 3

4. The best is option   because

Mediation Process
Keep Positive, Kind And Respectful!

Step 1

The mediator agrees not to take sides.
The mediator agrees not to offer any solutions.
The students agree to speak one at a time
and not interrupt each other.
They agree to show respect.
No blaming or accusations.

Step 2

The mediator asks each student in turn to
describe the problem and how they feel without interrupting each other.
The mediator summarises what each one says.

Step 3

The mediator asks each student to describe how the other one feels.

Step 4

The mediator asks each student for suggestions regarding 'How can we sort it out'?

Step 5

The mediator asks the students to agree a solution.

Work in 3s and use the 5-step process to 'act out' mediations for the following 6 problems:

1 Friends falling out over borrowed clothes – one friend has not returned the items and ruined one of them.	2 One person feels left out when he isn't invited to his friend's party because he gets bad-tempered when he drinks.	3 One friend has a new boyfriend/girlfriend and doesn't have time for his/her 'old' friend.
4 One person has been bullying his/her friend because of jealousy of the way he/she looks and dresses.	5 Friends falling out over money – one friend is always broke and forever borrowing money and not paying it back.	6 Friends falling out over drugs. One person likes to use cannabis and the other person thinks it's stupid and will result in paranoid behaviour.

CODING WITH PEER PRESSURE

1 What is it?

Discuss 'What is peer pressure?' What is your definition? Work in pairs and feed back. How are you definitions similar and different?

WORK IN PAIRS

2 What do you think?

Many people say that peer pressure is responsible for what they do, e.g. young people claiming they tried drugs because of peer pressure.

- Give examples of peer pressure which you have seen or felt?
- Why do people give in to peer pressure?

WORK IN GROUPS

KEY WORDS PEER PRESSURE - SPOKEN PRESSURE - REJECTION - PU

3 What about you?

Think back to the kinds of peer pressure you identified in the last activity. Were these 'spoken' or 'unspoken' pressures?

Look at the list of spoken and unspoken pressures below and think of times when you may have (a) used this kind of peer pressure and (b) been on the receiving end of this kind of peer pressure.

Spoken pressure
- Rejection – threatening to leave someone out/end a relationship.
- Put down – insulting/calling someone names to make them feel bad/sad.
- Reasoning – giving reasons why it would be okay to do a particular thing.

INDIVIDUAL SELF-REFLECTION ACTIVITY

Unspoken pressure
- The gang – a gang stands together talking/laughing, possibly at something you can't see and with their backs to you.
- The 'look' – students who think they are cool give you the look that says you're not one of us.
- The example – popular students will wear or buy something and everyone else will want to follow their example.

4 Activity

The best way to stand up to unwanted or negative peer pressure is to be assertive. Use assertive body language and 'I' statements in order to stand up to the following pressures. Working in pairs, develop a script for dealing with one of these pressures and then feedback. Which scripts sound most convincing and why?

WORK IN PAIRS

- To wear certain clothes which wouldn't suit you
- To have sex when you don't want to
- To take drugs
- To mess around in a lesson
- What to eat for lunch
- To have a cigarette
- Not to be a geek

5 Follow-on

- Complete the Peer Pressure Quiz on pages 50-51.

DOWN - UNSPOKEN PRESSURE - 'I' STATEMENTS - ASSERTIVENESS

Peer Pressure Quiz

1. You're at the local shop and you see one of your friends slip a pack of cigarettes into their pocket. You:
   a) pretend you didn't see them and look away.
   b) tell them that stealing is wrong and they should put it back before they're caught.
   c) decide that since they didn't get caught you might as well steal some too.
   Answer:

2. You're having an overnight party at your friend's house. While playing truth or dare, you are dared to drink half a bottle of vodka. You:
   a) open the bottle but at the last minute you decide to say no.
   b) say no and suggest a different activity.
   c) do it. You can't back down from a dare or you'll look soft.
   Answer:

3. While sitting at your lunch table, everyone starts laughing at your friend's new shoes as she goes up to get her lunch. You:
   a) sit there and eat your lunch and ignore it.
   b) join in. Your friend won't find out and you might be teased if you don't.
   c) stick up for your friend. How would they feel if their friends made fun of them?
   Answer:

4. You really want to go to a party at your girlfriend's house as you know you'll get some privacy. Your parents say "No way." Your best friend says he will help you get out by pretending you're going to his house instead. What do you do?
   a) Accept the offer and start getting ready.
   b) Stay home and make the best of it as you're still under age anyway.
   c) End up staying home but fight with your parents about it.
   Answer:

5. You're out with some friends when one of them lights a joint and offers you one. You:
   a) tell them you don't smoke joints and walk away.
   b) accept – it looks cool and you don't want to be left out.
   c) decline the offer. You don't need to do drugs to have fun.
   Answer:

6. Have you ever given into a peer pressure situation?
   a) Often
   b) Sometimes
   c) Never
   Answer:

7. It's Friday night. All of your friends are going to a party but you promised your little sister you would take her bowling. You:
   a) cancel your sister. You want to have fun!
   b) tell your friends a promise is a promise and take your little sister for her treat.
   c) go bowling but meet up with your friends later.
   Answer:

8. In the French exam, your best friend asks to look at your answers. You:
   a) cover your answers so they can't see them.
   b) let them, but tell the teacher after class in case you get into trouble.
   c) let them, because someday you might need to do it too.
   Answer:

Your teacher will now give you the scores for each answer. What was your total score?

1–8

You haven't learned to stand up to peer pressure. You often make the wrong decisions because of other people's influence on you. You need to decide who you are really are. Don't just go along with the crowd – try to be your own boss! Use your brains!

9–16

You are still learning to cope with peer pressure. Sometimes you make your own choices, but sometimes you still let other people pressure and choose for you. Instead of just letting an issue pass, try taking a stand and tell everyone how you feel. Use your assertiveness skills! You will get on better if you stand up for what you believe in and don't give in to them.

17–24

You're a star! You know how to resist peer pressure. You are comfortable with what you believe and don't mind being different and not following what's popular. You are assertive and know how to stick up for yourself and what you believe in without hurting others. You can empathise and show respect for others, which is why they won't pressure you. Keep it up!!

The following are links which someone who is being subjected to peer pressure could find useful:
www.likeitis.org.uk/peerpressure.html
www.kidshealth.org/kid/feeling/peerpressure.html
www.iwannaknow.org/brain2/peerpressure.html

Focus on Solutions

1 What is it?

In order to protect our emotional and physical well-being we need to maintain a positive outlook on life. Being negative and looking at life in a negative way will only have negative consequences. We'll all have problems in our lives. What we need to do is develop our skills for finding solutions rather than focusing on the problems.

2 What do you think?

WORK IN GROUPS AND FEEDBACK

What are the 'negatives' of being a teenager? Work out positive responses to each of these.

3 Reframing

Sometimes there's a different way of looking at things that annoy us. This is called reframing. Try and 'reframe' each of the statements below into a positive statement. The first one has been done for you.

He's so lazy	Could be	He's laid back/relaxed
She's always nagging	Could be	
He's a loner	Could be	
She always interferes	Could be	
He's so in your face	Could be	
She has a high opinion of herself	Could be	
He's a swot	Could be	
She's really thick in maths	Could be	

Now think of the last negative thought you had about yourself. Then REFRAME IT!

KEY WORDS SOLUTIONS - SKILLS - STRATEGIES

4 Activity

WORK IN PAIRS

- With each of you using a mirror, draw your self-portraits.
- Then around the outside of your portrait write down all the skills and qualities you would like to have.
- Swap portraits. After seeing your partner's list, would you like to make any changes to your own list?
- Discuss each other's lists.

5 What about you?

What would your 'best future' look like? Try to visualise this! Describe it in detail using the following sentence starters:

- I will be
- I will have
- I will look like
- I will feel like
- I will be with
- I will live in

Record your 'best future' on a postcard, then look at it again in a few months' time.

6 Follow-on

- Complete the Miracle Question and Scaling Activity on pages 54-55.

POSITIVE STATEMENT - REFRAMING - TARGETS

The Miracle Question and Scaling Activity

Step 1

The Miracle Question

Imagine that you go to bed tonight and a miracle happens – a magic wand is waved over you and all your problems and difficulties are solved.

You wake up to a 'perfect day' at home and at school. Firstly, record your usual day. Then record your miraculous day. What's different? How does your day begin and then go on?

Then list the differences between a 'usual day' and a 'miraculous' day, and work out what you need to do in order to achieve a more positive outcome.

1. Usual Day	2. Miraculous Day
Morning	Morning
Afternoon	Afternoon
Evening	Evening

Step 2

If you want to move nearer to your miraculous day, you have to do something. Have a go at the scaling activity below and identify the things you can do to achieve this.

The Scaling Activity

1	2	3	4	5	6	7	8	9	10

Mark where you are now on the scale in terms of how positive you feel about your life and well-being at the moment (1 being the least positive and 10 being the most positive).

I am at point................

What have you done to get as far as that?

I have done these things:

•

•

•

•

What can you do to move higher up the scale? (Remember that your targets should be realistic.)

The things I can do are:

•

•

•

•

Now try and do these things.
Set yourself a review date when you will decide whether you have moved up the scale in your opinion.
N.B. Identify who can help you along the way.